COMPOSER SHOWCASE
HAL LEONARD STUDENT PIANO LIBRARY

T0056006

Watercolor Miniatures

BY CAROL KLOSE

CONTENTS

ISBN 978-1-61780-539-4

HAL•LEONARD®
CORPORATION

7777 W. BLUEMOUND RD. P.O. BOX 13819 MILWAUKEE, WI 53213

In Australia Contact:
Hal Leonard Australia Pty. Ltd.
4 Lentara Court
Cheltenham, Victoria, 3192 Australia
Email: ausadmin@halleonard.com.au

Visit Hal Leonard Online at
www.halleonard.com

Fireflies on a Summer Night

for Mary

By Carol Klose

Flitting (♩ = 160-176)

Hold damper pedal down throughout

Repeat ad lib., starting very fast and light as a tremolo, becoming softer and slower, fading into the F♯ at the end.

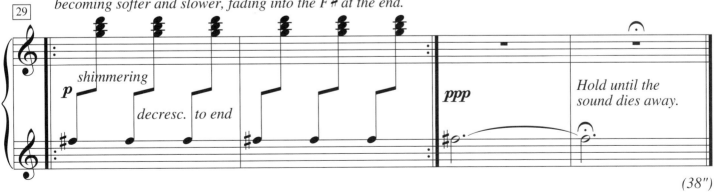

(38″)

Fawn in the Magical Forest

for Ann

By Carol Klose

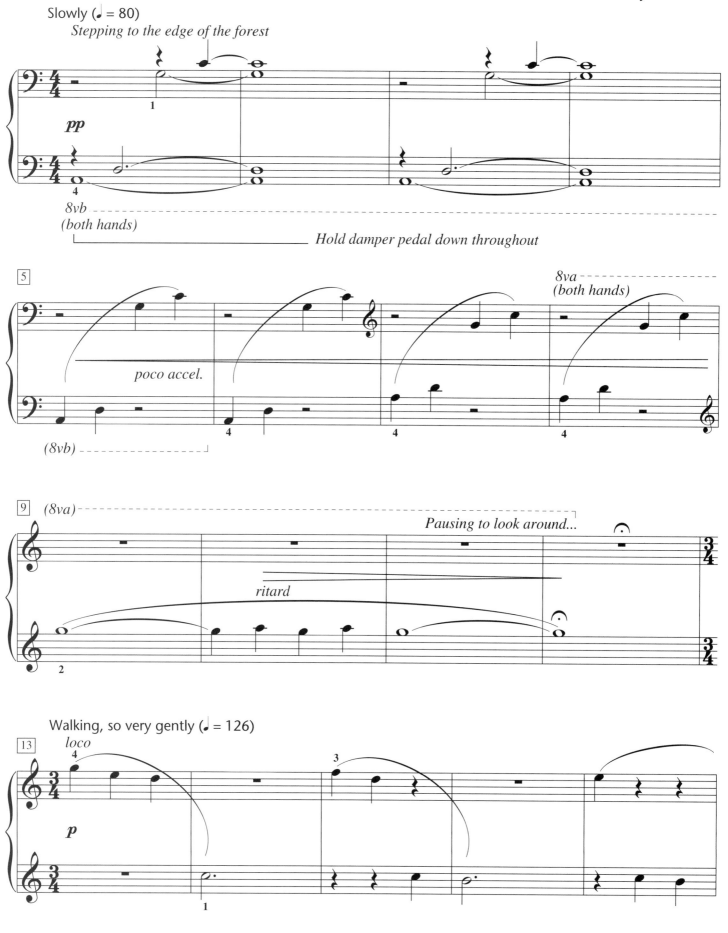

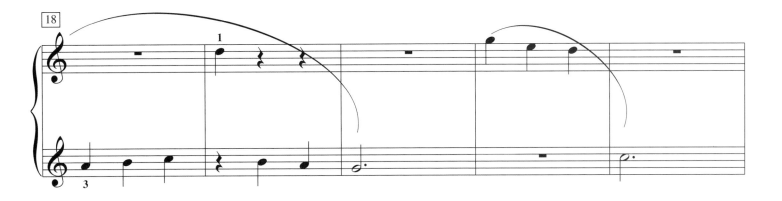

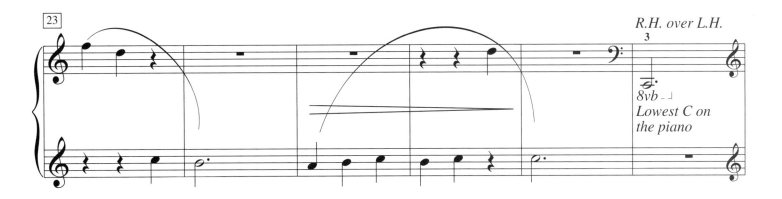

R.H. over L.H.

8vb
Lowest C on
the piano

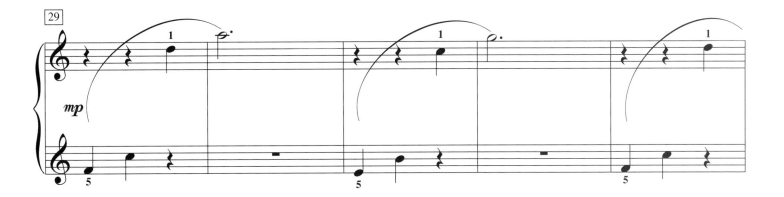

mp

mf

5

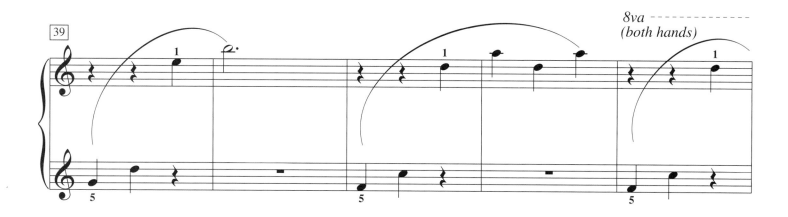

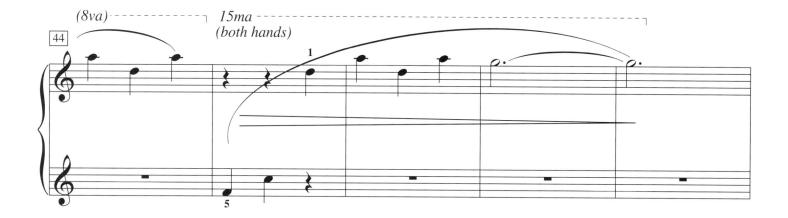

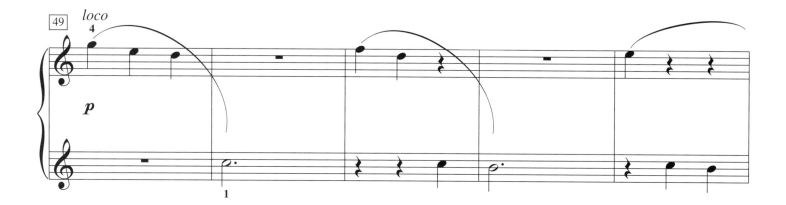

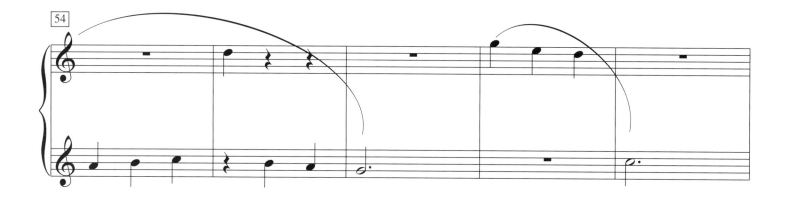

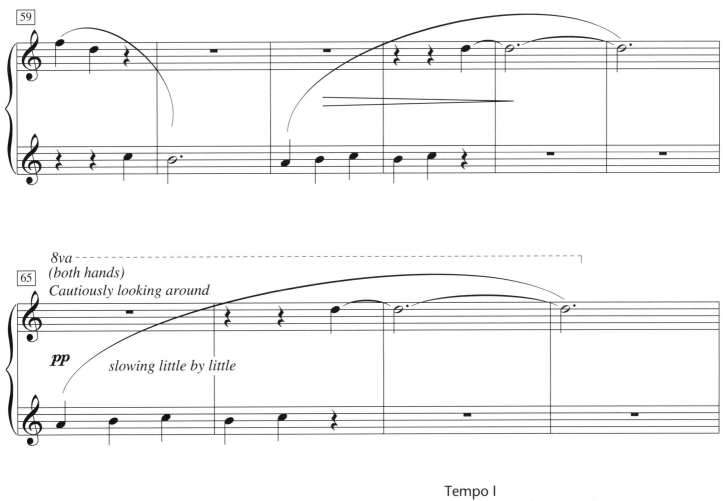

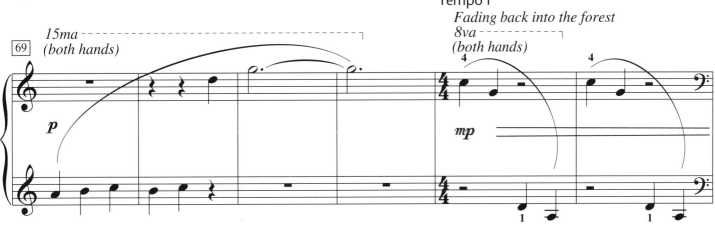

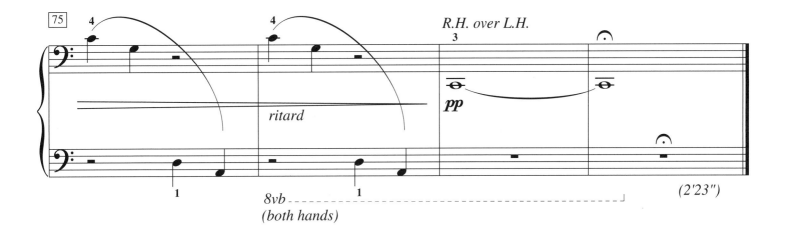

Ancient Towers

for Alex

By Carol Klose

Slowly, with majestic mystery (♩ = 69)

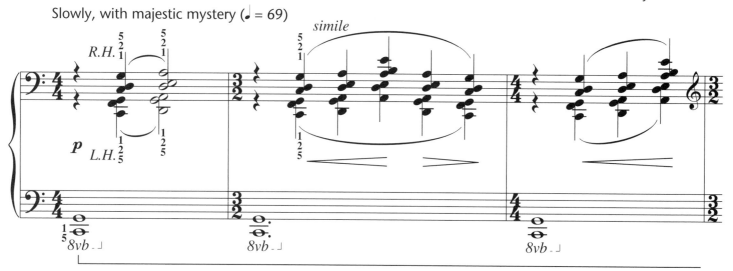

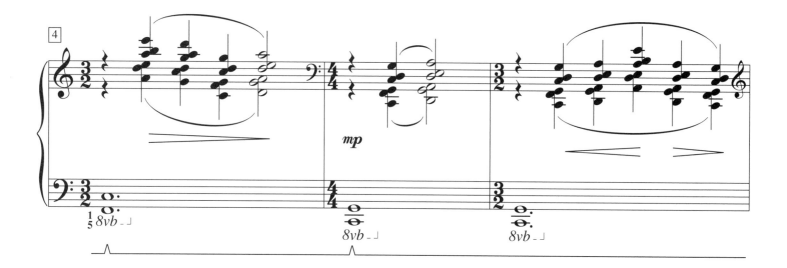

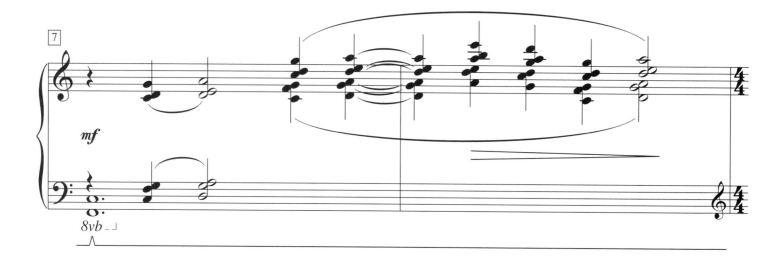

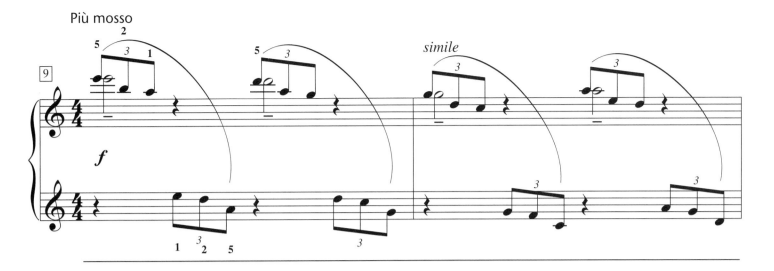

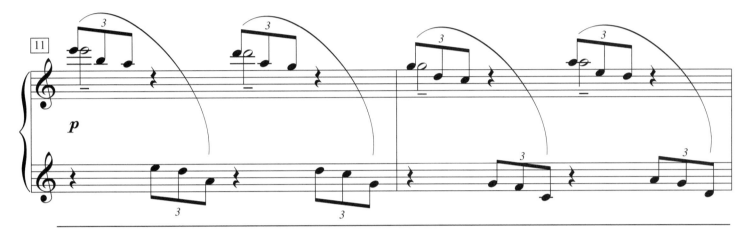

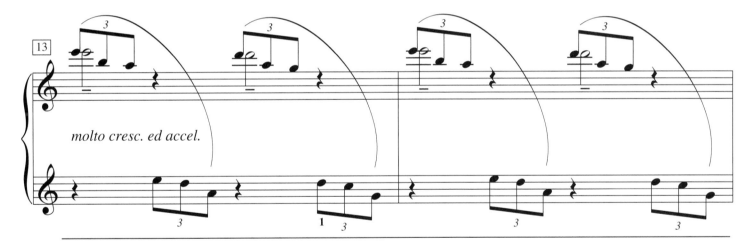

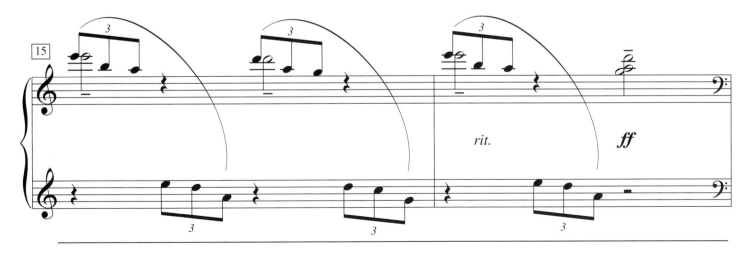

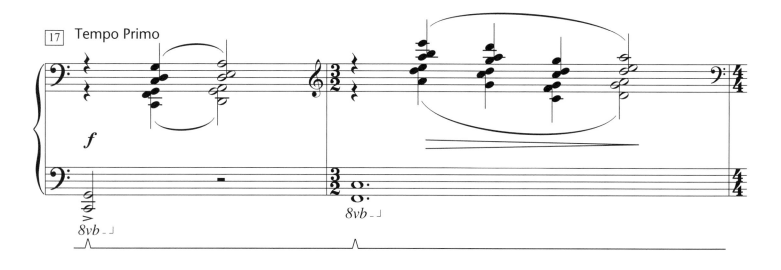

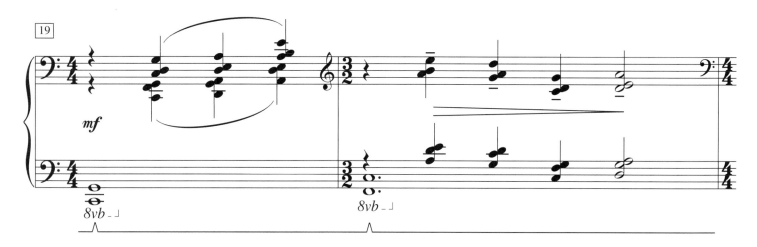

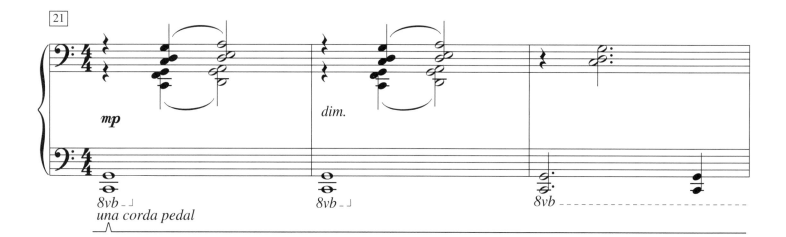

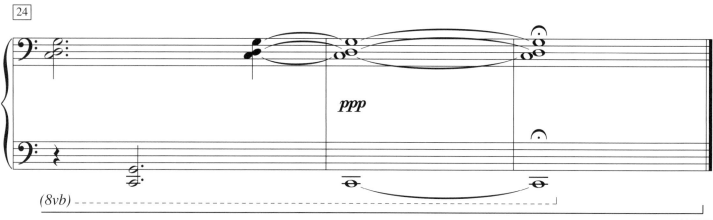

(1'43")

The Blue Cocoon

for Katherine

By Carol Klose

Slowly, just hangin' out (straight 8ths) (♩ = 92)

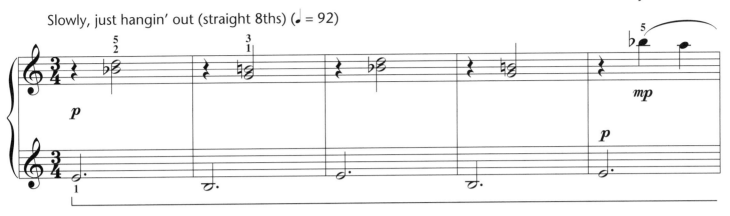

R.H. over L.H.

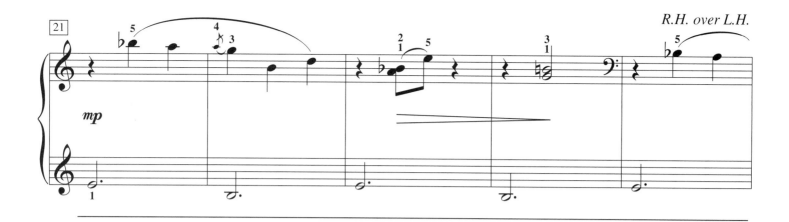

cresc. poco a poco

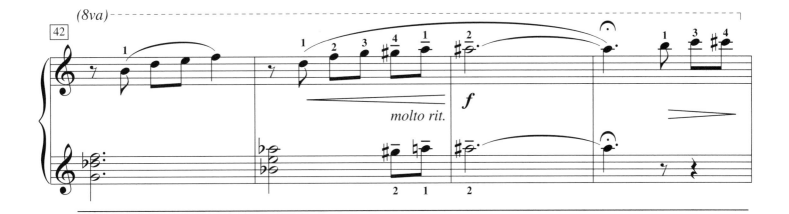

molto rit. f

Gaily ($\bullet$ = 152)

8va (both hands)

mp *leggiero*

(8va)

quickly, as if fluttering away (no rit.)

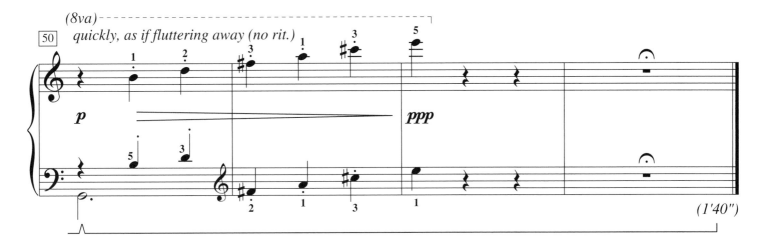

p ppp

(1'40")

Dreaming in Watercolors

for Maddie

By Carol Klose

Flowing, as if painting freely on a canvas (in "2") ($\textstyle\quad$ = 66-72)

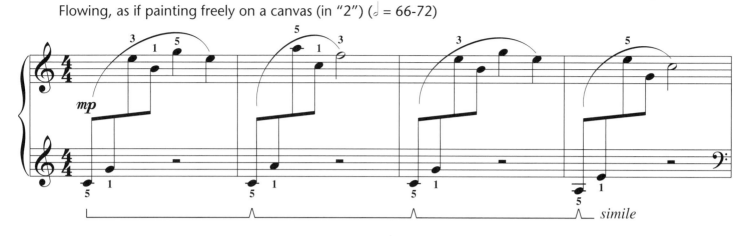

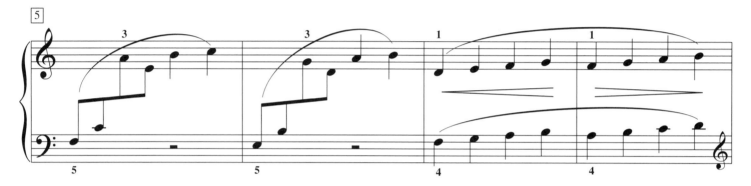

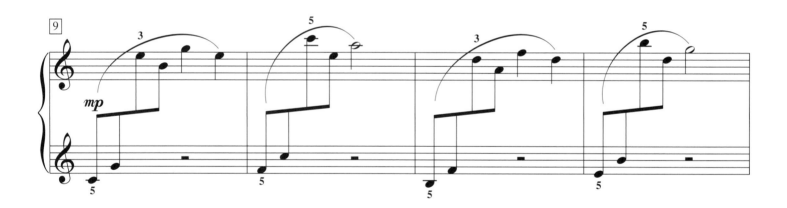

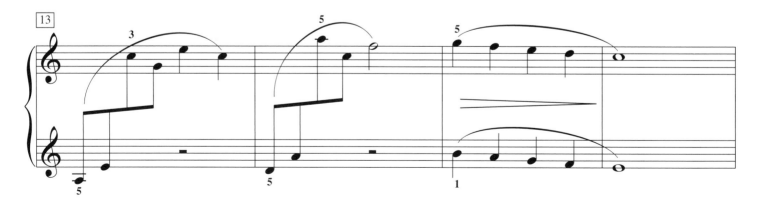

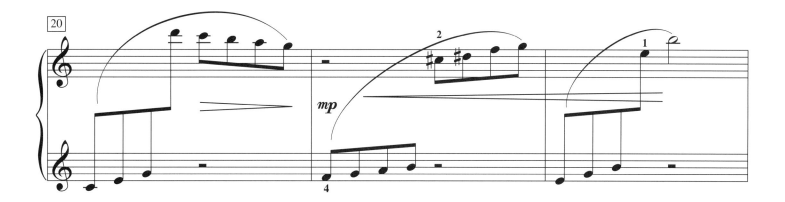

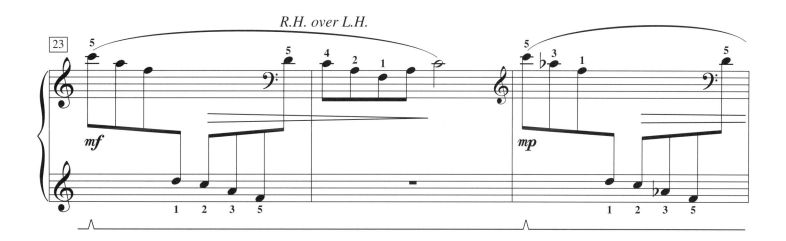

R.H. over L.H.

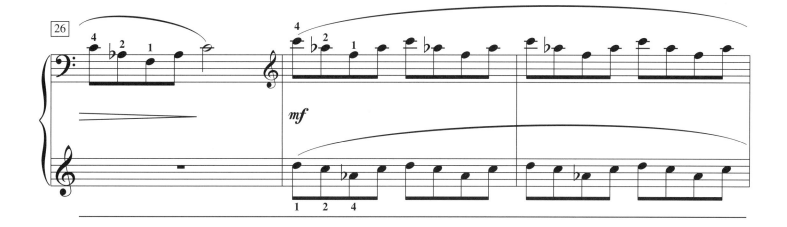

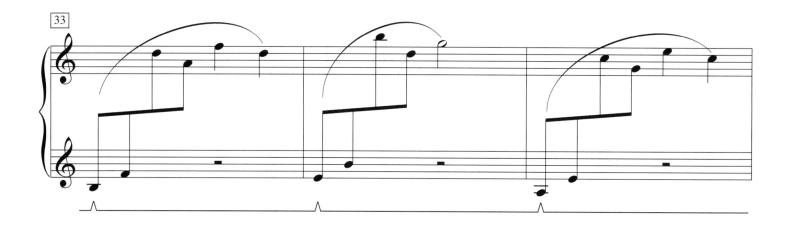

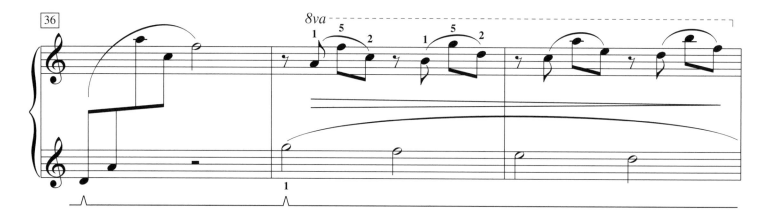

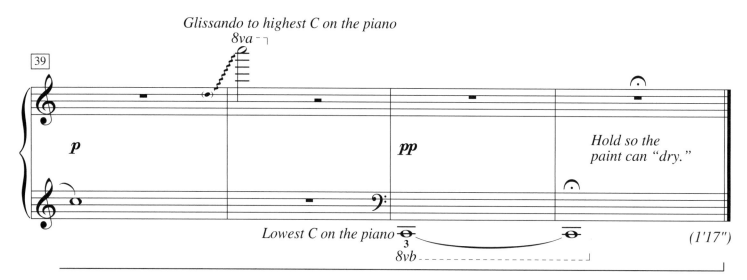

Sea Otter Splash

for Renée

By Carol Klose

Lively, full of zip, in "2" (♩ = 104-116)

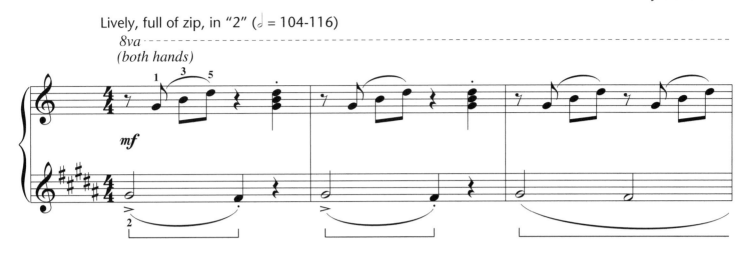

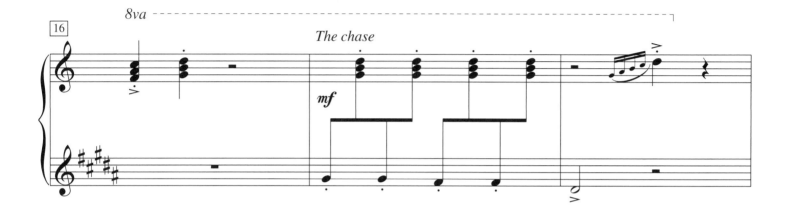

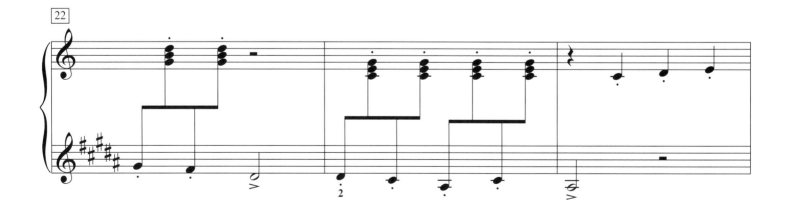

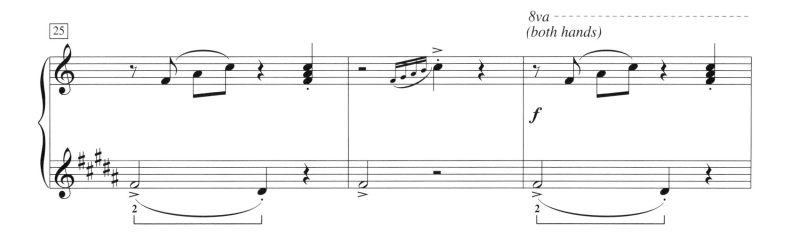

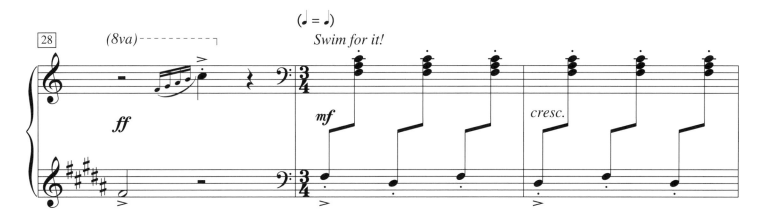

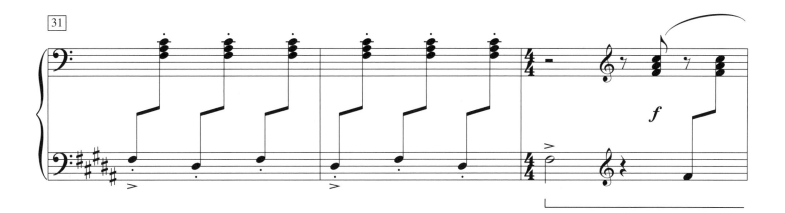

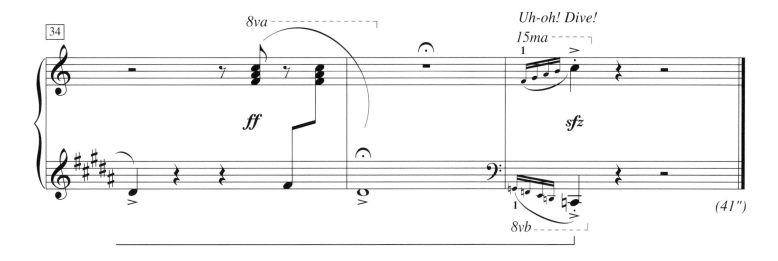

Gathering Storm Clouds

for Jane

By Carol Klose

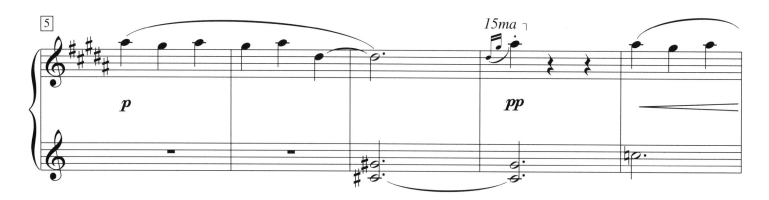

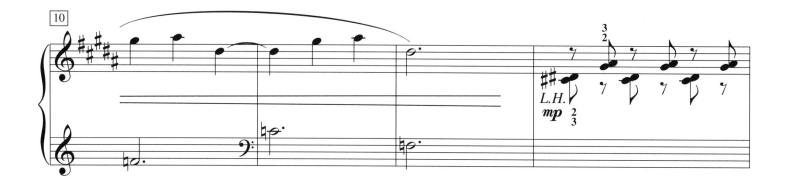

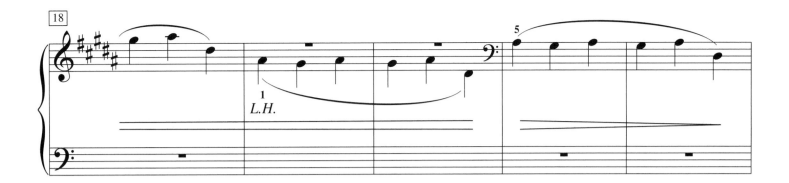

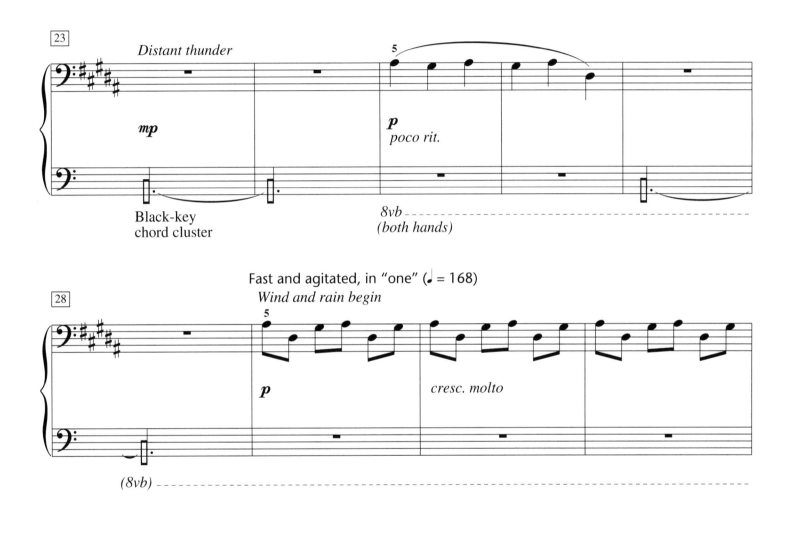

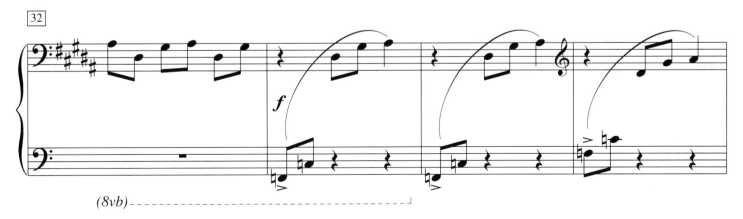

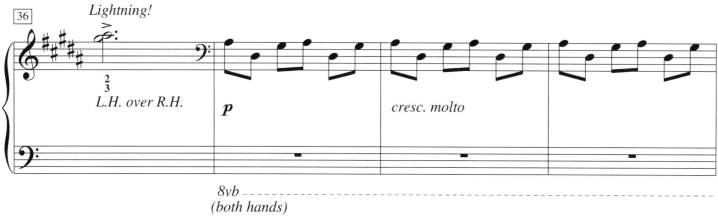

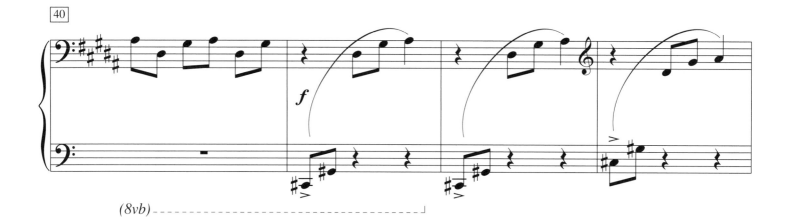

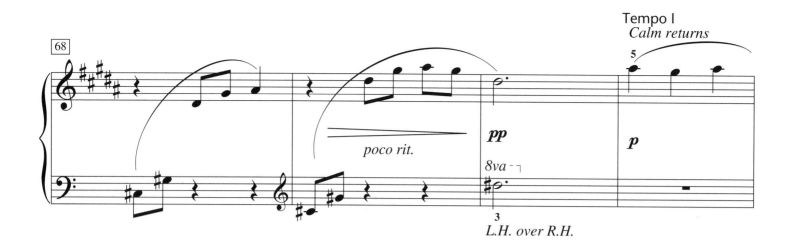

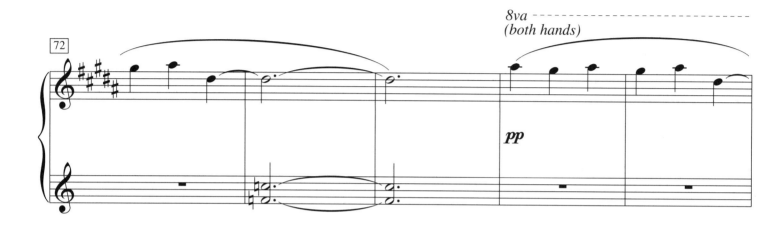

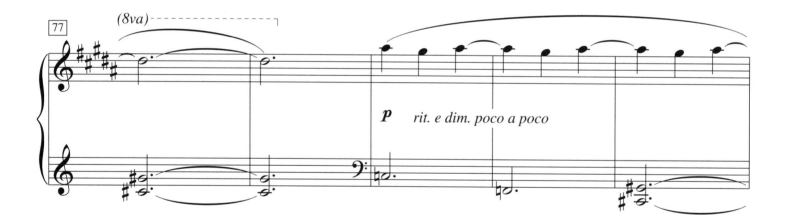

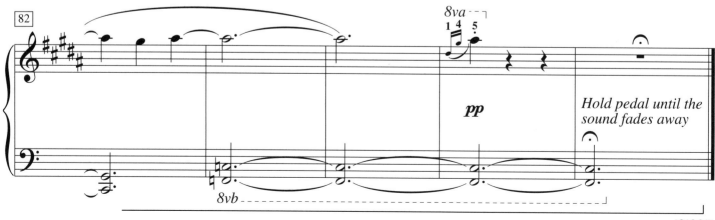

(2'00")